Civics in Colorado

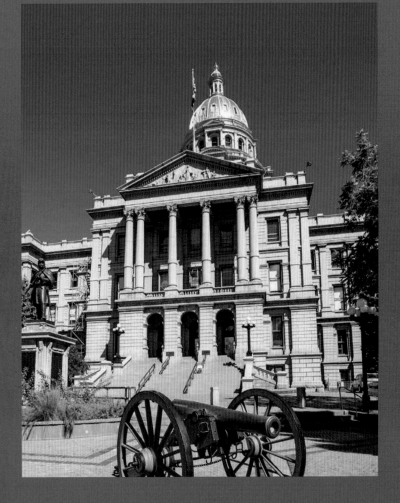

Elise Wallace

Table of Contents

Chapter 1

The Start of the State

Colorado is a state with many nicknames. The state flower is the Columbine, so it has been called the Columbine State. It has been called the Lead State. Lead is a metal found in the state. It has been called the Highest State too. This is because it has many mountain peaks. But one of its nicknames is more famous than the rest. This nickname is as old as the state itself.

Colorado became a state during a key year. That year was 1876. Now, think back 100 years earlier to 1776. An important document was signed that year. It changed the course of history. It was called the Declaration of Independence.

This is where Colorado's official nickname comes from. Colorado is known as the **Centennial** State. The word *centennial* is used to describe the 100th anniversary of something. Colorado became a state on the nation's 100th anniversary. It was the 38th state to join the Union.

The Highest State

The Rocky Mountains help make Colorado the tallest state. The average altitude of the state is more than a mile above sea level.

Black Hawk, a historic mining city

The Colorado Territory

The United States **acquired** Colorado's land through two events. The first was the Louisiana Purchase. In 1803, the U.S. government bought land from France. It was a lot of land. Today, this land makes up parts of 15 different states. This is how Colorado got its eastern land.

The second event was a war. It was between the United States and Mexico. Mexico *ceded*, or was forced to give up, some of its land. Mexico gave it to the United States. This is how Colorado got its western land.

People started to move to the area. They were looking for gold. In 1858, gold was found near Pikes Peak. That year, the capital city of Denver was founded. A few years later, the Colorado Territory was formed. This was in 1861.

Louisiana Purchase territory

Hunting for Gold

Colorado was a popular area during the gold rush. Pikes Peak was a key landmark for people coming west. During the gold rush, people created the slogan "Pikes Peak or Bust!"

Colorado's Government

The road to statehood was a long one. It took many years of hard work.

Many statehood **bills** were written. They were sent to the U.S. Congress again and again. For years, none of them passed. Then, President Ulysses S. Grant signed the Enabling Act in 1875. This meant that Colorado could become a state. They just needed an approved **constitution**. This explains how a state or country should be governed.

So, one was written. The public voted and approved it. In 1876, Colorado became a state.

Colorado's government was modeled after the U.S. government. It has the same three branches. Each branch has its own leaders. These leaders have unique duties. They serve different roles in the state.

Ulysses S. Grant, 18th president of the United States

Your Vote, Your Voice

U.S. citizens can vote when they turn 18. Voting can be done in person at polling centers. Voting can also be done by mail. It's important to vote. It's a great way to get involved.

Executive Branch

The leader of the state's executive branch is the governor. The governor is elected by the public. They have many jobs. One of them is to **enforce** state laws. The governor can also pass or **veto** laws. There are also other leaders in this branch. The secretary of state is in charge of state elections and voting. The state treasurer manages the state's money. This money comes from taxes that people pay. These are taxes such as income and sales tax.

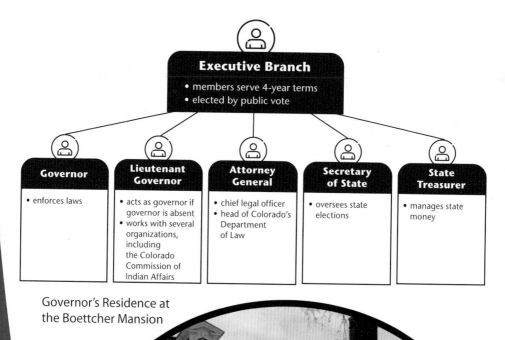

Executive Branch
- members serve 4-year terms
- elected by public vote

Governor
- enforces laws

Lieutenant Governor
- acts as governor if governor is absent
- works with several organizations, including the Colorado Commission of Indian Affairs

Attorney General
- chief legal officer
- head of Colorado's Department of Law

Secretary of State
- oversees state elections

State Treasurer
- manages state money

Governor's Residence at the Boettcher Mansion

Members of the Colorado General Assembly gather for a session at the state capitol.

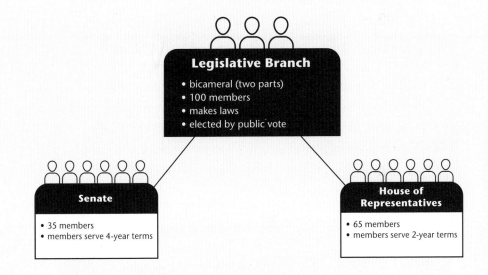

Legislative Branch
- bicameral (two parts)
- 100 members
- makes laws
- elected by public vote

Senate
- 35 members
- members serve 4-year terms

House of Representatives
- 65 members
- members serve 2-year terms

Legislative Branch

There are two parts to the legislative branch. One part is the Senate. The other part is the House of Representatives. These two parts together are called the General Assembly. This branch votes on bills. They decide whether bills should become laws. This branch also approves the state budget.

Judicial Branch

This branch **interprets** the law. It decides the meanings of laws. It also decides whether people have broken laws. The judicial branch is made up of many courts. These include the supreme court and the court of appeals. The court of appeals looks at past trials. They decide if a trial's results were fair. The state supreme court hears cases that have been appealed by all other courts.

The leader of this branch is the chief justice. The chief justice chooses the chief judge. The chief judge leads the court of appeals.

Federal, State, and Local

The three branches of the state government work together to serve the people. They make new laws and make sure those laws are enforced. The state government also works with federal and local governments. These three levels of government provide many services.

Colorado supreme court justices

The state supreme court meets in this courtroom in the Ralph L. Carr Colorado Judicial Center.

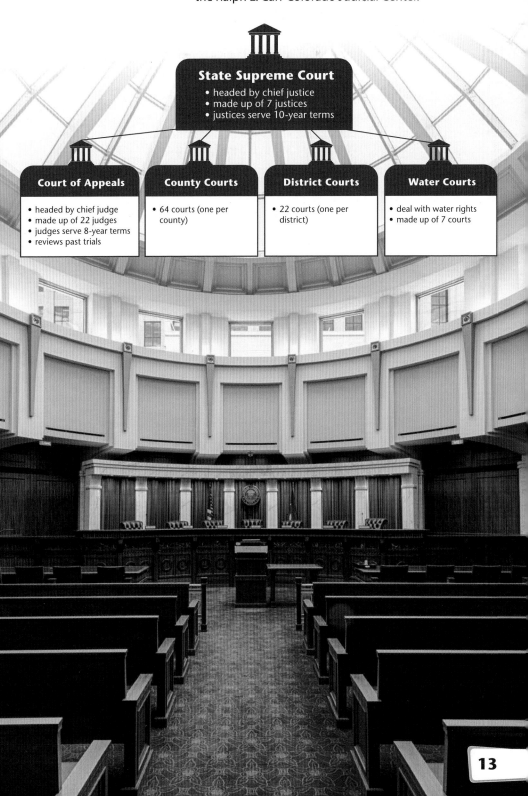

State Supreme Court
- headed by chief justice
- made up of 7 justices
- justices serve 10-year terms

Court of Appeals
- headed by chief judge
- made up of 22 judges
- judges serve 8-year terms
- reviews past trials

County Courts
- 64 courts (one per county)

District Courts
- 22 courts (one per district)

Water Courts
- deal with water rights
- made up of 7 courts

State and federal governments have a lot in common. They provide some of the same services. They both deal with health care, schools, and roads. These services are funded through taxes. Taxes help pay for government spending. They also pay for public services.

Local governments have services too. These include local police and fire departments. Cities or towns receive money from both state and federal governments. They also get money from taxes.

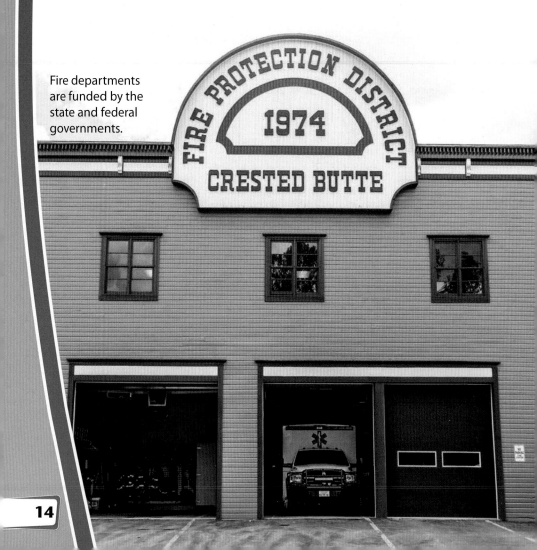

Fire departments are funded by the state and federal governments.

Public schools are a service provided by the government.

Local, state, and federal governments need to work together on many policies. One of them is education. State and federal governments give money to schools. They make sure that schools follow the law. But it is up to local governments to manage schools.

Another example of this teamwork is roads. The federal government takes care of interstate highways, such as I-70. It goes all the way to Maryland. The state government takes care of highways that are only in the state. All three levels of government have to work together. They ensure that people's needs are met.

Get Involved

People like you can create change! In 1996, a group of fourth graders argued that the Colorado Hairstreak butterfly should be the official state insect. Legislators agreed.

Chapter 2

Issues in the State

Every state deals with issues. Some of these issues are the same from state to state. Most states face challenges, such as climate change and health care. Crime and traffic can also be problems. These issues are often different in each state. For example, states with fewer people may not have as much traffic.

Colorado has many issues to solve. Two big issues are energy and health care. People in Colorado work together on these issues. They try to find solutions.

Nonrenewable Resources

Natural gas and coal take millions of years for nature to make. They are called **fossil fuels**. They are made from the remains of ancient plants and animals.

This bill has the goal of reducing greenhouse gas emissions. These emissions are partially caused by burning coal and natural gas. They cause climate change. They can also cause pollution.

People outside the government work to get bills passed too. These groups **collaborate** with lawmakers. They argue for bills that **promote** clean energy. Their influence has resulted in new laws. These laws protect the environment.

New energy laws are passed each year. One law promotes the use of electric cars. It gives tax credits to electric car owners. That means the government pays for some of their taxes. This is an **incentive** for many Coloradans. This law helps protect the environment.

Lawmakers in Colorado have energy goals. They want to make energy use more **efficient**. Some laws require home appliances to meet certain standards. These standards help lower the amount of energy that is used to run appliances.

It is becoming more common to find charging stations for electric cars in parking lots.

ELECTRIC VEHICLE PARKING ONLY

People in communities can get involved too. One thing you can do is contact members of the state government. They can be reached by phone or through email. Another way is to find a group that shares your passion. There are many groups to choose from. One of the best ways to make positive changes is to work with others.

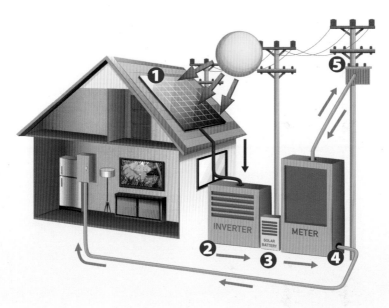

1. solar panels

2. solar inverter

3. solar battery

4. digital meter connected to an electric panel

5. excess energy pushed out to the power grid

Storing Energy

Solar energy can only be collected during the day. It is expensive to store as well. There needs to be an efficient way to store it. This is a problem the state (and the world) needs to solve.

Health Care

Another big issue that people in Colorado want to address is health care. There are a lot of people who think that it costs too much. Some people cannot afford to get the care they need. Others are struggling to pay for medication.

The state is trying to lower the cost of health care. It is doing this in many ways. There are new laws that address the problem. One law helps insurance companies pay for patients' most expensive claims. This will help save patients money. Another law keeps the cost of medicine down. This law focuses solely on reducing the price of insulin. This is a medicine for people with diabetes. In some places, insulin can cost hundreds of dollars each month.

Children's Hospital Colorado in Aurora

Colorado is working to keep insulin affordable.

Where Does the Money Go?

When people pay for medical services, the money goes to different places. Some goes to insurance companies. Most of it goes to doctors and hospitals.

Patients can be surprised by how much it costs to go to the hospital. Their visits can cost a lot of money. So, lawmakers passed a new bill. The bill's goal is to help lower surprise costs. These are hidden fees that people do not know about until they get home.

Health care issues are complex. So, they are not easily solved. People inside and outside of the government still have work to do. It is important that health care is affordable. People need it to stay safe and healthy.

Costly Care

U.S. citizens spend a lot of money on health care. Johns Hopkins University researched this. They learned that Americans pay more money than people in other developed countries.

Energy and health care are just two issues that Colorado faces. Both of them require deep thinking. They also require participation. People can help raise awareness of these issues in many ways. They can hold meetings and talk to others. They can also design posters or even create websites.

An easy way to raise awareness of an issue is to create a sign or poster.

Chapter 3

Civic Engagement

Some people may think that they need to work for the government to cause change. But this is not the case! People outside the government can cause change too. Many people can affect how issues are solved. They can vote for people they agree with. They can protest ideas they don't like. They can speak up for the ideas they are passionate about. People like you can affect how the state is run by joining groups and raising awareness.

But these are not the only ways to cause change. There is still more to learn about **civic** engagement. Every person can make positive changes in Colorado. Many people are changemakers in their towns, cities, and counties. Two Coloradans who have gone above and beyond for their state are Will Toor and Kate Greenberg.

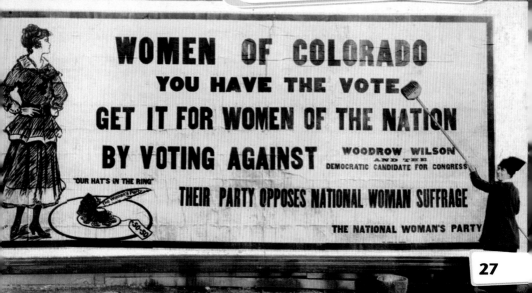

Give Us the Vote!

Voting is a big part of civic engagement. Wyoming gave women the right to vote in 1869. Colorado was next. It gave women the right to vote in 1893.

A 1916 billboard encouraged women to vote.

WOMEN OF COLORADO
YOU HAVE THE VOTE
GET IT FOR WOMEN OF THE NATION
BY VOTING AGAINST WOODROW WILSON AND THE DEMOCRATIC CANDIDATE FOR CONGRESS

"OUR HAT'S IN THE RING"

THEIR PARTY OPPOSES NATIONAL WOMAN SUFFRAGE

THE NATIONAL WOMAN'S PARTY

Will Toor

Will Toor is a changemaker. For decades, Toor has worked to improve life in Colorado. He was the mayor of Boulder for six years. Toor started a group called Better Boulder. It supports people who want to build affordable housing in the city. Another one of Toor's key roles was in state government. He has been the head of the Colorado Energy Office.

Will Toor

Toor wants Colorado to use more clean energy. He has always practiced what he preaches. He has an electric car. He has solar electricity at his house.

Toor works with others to meet his goals. He encourages people on different sides of an issue to work together. Not everyone agrees with him. But this never stopped him! Throughout his life, he has spoken up for the use of clean energy.

aerial view of Boulder

Saving Energy

There are simple things everyone can do at home to save energy. It's a good idea to turn off lights when you're not home. Turning off the air conditioner helps too. This way, both energy and money are saved.

Kate Greenberg

Kate Greenberg has always had a heart for farmers. She has worked with them across the country. Her work as head of the Colorado state department of agriculture has made a huge difference. The person in this role fights for the rights of farmers. They lead the department.

Greenberg is interested in **conservation**. This means protecting resources. Farmers need to be able to access many resources. These resources should be used efficiently too. Sustainable farming can help. This type of farming protects the environment. It also helps protect the future of farming.

Greenberg has traveled around the state. She has met with ranchers and farmers. She has listened to their problems. Many farmers in the state have struggles. They are dealing with climate change and lack of water. Greenberg has helped address their needs.

Kate Greenberg

This farmer works on his vegetables on Rock Ledge Ranch in Colorado Springs.

Better Farming

Sustainable farming uses different methods. One of them is crop rotation. This helps the soil keep key nutrients. Soil needs enough of these nutrients so crops can grow.

Will Toor and Kate Greenberg are great examples of civic engagement. They have both created positive change in the state. They have followed their passions to make Colorado better. Their work will have lasting impacts.

Making a Change

Colorado is a state made of changemakers. Everyone has the ability to create change. Think about where Colorado should be in the future. What should we do better? How do we get there? It's important to work toward a better future for all Coloradans.

State laws are not set in stone. So, Colorado is constantly changing. Just take a look at the state's constitution. It has been changed more than a hundred times!

Young Trailblazer

Mirabai Herz is making Colorado better. She helps maintain trails throughout the state. Herz wants to help others enjoy outdoor spaces. She wants to keep them safe while they do so.

Chapter 4

Casimiro Barela:
An Advocate for Change

Colorado's state history is filled with changemakers. One of them is Casimiro Barela. He was a state senator for 37 years. He helped write the state's constitution.

Barela was born in Mexico. When he was a young man, he moved to the Colorado Territory. He settled near the city of Trinidad.

Barela soon found a new passion. It was politics. Barela became a justice of the peace. This is a person who deals with local disputes. As the years passed, Barela worked many jobs in and out of politics. He was a jack-of-all-trades. Barela was a sheriff and a county assessor. He worked as a postmaster too. There was nothing he couldn't do!

Casimiro Barela
(1847–1920)

A Turning Point

Barela was born during the middle of a war. He was born in the area that is present-day New Mexico. At the time, this land was a part of Mexico. Less than a year later, that land belonged to the United States.

Barela made history. He was part of a key group of people. They were the ones who wrote the state constitution.

Barela was proud of what they wrote. He wanted everyone in Colorado to read it. So, he argued that it should be translated. People listened. The constitution was written in English. Then, it was translated into Spanish and German.

Soon, Barela became a state senator. He worked hard for the public good. Many people respected him. For decades, he was reelected. Barela was a voice for the voiceless. He bravely fought for the rights of others.

Barela supported causes that were not popular at the time. He argued for women's right to vote. He fought for the rights of Latino ranchers. He fought for the rights of Italian miners too. Barela was unique. He truly was one of the state's greats.

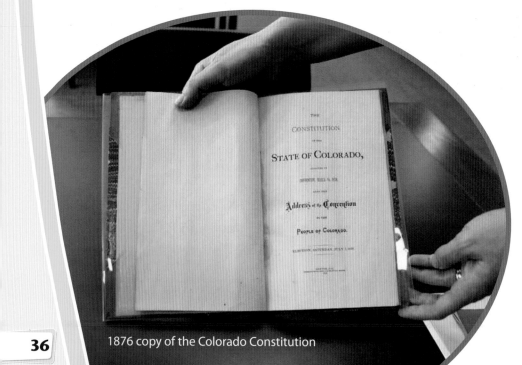

1876 copy of the Colorado Constitution

Barela's portrait in the capitol

A Lasting Legacy

Barela made a lasting impact on Colorado. People want to remember him. He was honored at the capitol building. There is a portrait of him there.

Glossary

acquired—had come to own something

bills—new laws that are suggested; the lawmakers of a country or state must vote to accept them before they become laws

centennial—the 100th anniversary of something

civic—relating to citizenship or being a citizen

collaborate—to work with another person or group to achieve or do something

conservation—carefully protecting and preserving resources

constitution—the system of beliefs and laws by which a country, state, or organization is governed

efficient—capable of producing desired results without wasting materials, time, or energy

emissions—things that are sent out or given off, such as energy or gases

enforce—to make sure that people do what is required by law

fossil fuels—fuels such as coal, oil, and natural gas that are formed in the earth from dead plants or animals

incentive—something that encourages a person to do something or to work harder

interprets—to explain the meaning of something

nonrenewable—not able to grow again or be made again, not able to be replaced by nature

promote—to help something happen, develop, or increase

renewable—able to be replaced by nature

sustainable—able to be used without being completely used up or destroyed

veto—a decision by a person in authority to not approve something, such as a new law

Index

Civics in Your Community

Colorado faces many issues. You have read about a few, such as energy and health care. The state also deals with crime, traffic, and homelessness.

Choose an issue in Colorado. Research how it is addressed by your community. Does your community have laws related to the issue? Are there local groups devoted to the issue? How do you think the issue should be resolved?

1. Make a graphic that compares three points of view on the issue. Your opinion should be one of the viewpoints, and the opinion of a member of your local government should be another. (The internet is a good resource for finding government members' stances on issues.)

2. Ask a classmate for their thoughts. Then, add their feedback to the graphic as a third point of view.

3. Review your work. Then, design a poster to showcase the issue. Take a stance on the issue. What should be done to fix it?